Communities at Work™

Community Resources
The Land and the People
in Communities

Angela Catalano

The Rosen Publishing Group's
PowerKids Press™
New York

For Mom and Dad for the past thirty-four years.
And for Frank, for the next thirty-four years—and beyond!

Published in 2005 by The Rosen Publishing Group, Inc.
29 East 21st Street, New York, NY 10010

First Edition

Editor: Natashya Wilson
Book Design: Maria E. Melendez
Layout Design: Albert B. Hanner

Photo Credits: Cover, p. 1 © Robert E Daemmrich/Getty Images; p. 5 © Jose Luis Pelaez, Inc./CORBIS; p. 7 © John MacPherson/CORBIS; p. 9 © Ariel Skelley/CORBIS; p. 11 © Tim McGuire/CORBIS; p. 13 © Bill Ross/CORBIS; p. 15 © Bill Miles/CORBIS; p. 17 © Peter Beck/CORBIS; p. 19 © David Turnley/CORBIS; p. 21 © David Pollack/CORBIS.

Library of Congress Cataloging-in-Publication Data

Catalano, Angela.
Community resources : the land and the people in communities / Angela Catalano.— 1st ed.
    v. cm. — (Communities at work)
Includes bibliographical references and index.
Contents: Community resources — Natural resources — Human resources — Capital resources — A city — A suburb — The country — Sharing resources — A school community — People helping the community.
ISBN 1-4042-2781-4 (library binding) — ISBN 1-4042-5016-6 (pbk.)
1. Community life—United States—Juvenile literature. 2. Community organization—United States—Juvenile literature. 3. Social service—United States—Juvenile literature. [1. Community life. 2. Social service.] I. Title. II. Series.

HM761.C38 2005
307'.0973—dc22

2003023267

Manufactured in the United States of America

Contents

Community Resources

A community is any place in which people live and work together. Schools, towns, and cities are examples of communities.

Communities have needs, such as food and housing for people. A community meets its needs with **resources**. A resource is something of value. Water, jobs, and tools are resources.

Students and teachers are part of a school community. Schools are full of resources. Teachers are resources. Chairs, books, and art supplies are resources. Students are also resources!

Natural Resources

A **natural resource** is anything found in nature that has not been changed by people. Forests, rivers, and animals are examples of natural resources. People often choose to build communities in areas that have many natural resources. The natural resources supply the community with homes, food, and jobs.

Forests are natural resources. The trees of the forest are used for making goods such as homes, paper, and tables. Some people have jobs cutting down trees and making goods from them.

Human Resources

People work and produce **goods** and **services** for the community. People who create goods and services are called **human resources**. For example, police officers and firefighters supply a service. They keep communities safe.

Children are human resources, too. Their job is to go to school. When they grow up, they will use what they have learned to help their communities.

Firefighters supply services. They help to keep communities safe from fire. They also teach people how to be safe around fire.

Capital Resources

Anything made by people that is used to create a good or a service is called a **capital resource**. When people work to produce goods and services for the community, they use capital resources. Tools, buildings, and computers are examples of capital resources.

Capital resources can be used again and again until they wear out. Hammers and other tools are some capital resources that are used to build houses. ▷

Cities

Millions of people live and work in cities. Cities are called **urban** communities. Cities need many resources. People in cities need food, water, clothing, and houses.

Cities are full of working people, so they have many human and capital resources. Many cities were started because natural resources were close by.

New York City is next to two rivers and an ocean. When the city began, people traveled by boat. They also shipped goods by boat. Many people came to New York City because it is easy to get to by boat.

Traveling to and from work every day is called commuting. Some people commute by car. Other people commute by train or bus. People who commute are called commuters.

Suburbs

A **suburban** community is one that is close to a city. A city may have many suburbs.

Cities and their suburbs often share human resources. Many people who live in suburbs work in the nearby city. Cities and suburbs may also share natural resources, such as a water supply.

Many people who live in the suburbs take a train to and from the city for work each day. The train is a capital resource.

The Country

A **rural** community is one that is found in the country, where there is farmland. Rural communities have many natural resources.

Many people in rural communities grow their own food and raise animals. These communities often sell their goods to other communities.

Rural communities have plenty of land. Many farmers grow crops. They sell their crops to suburban and urban communities. This farmer and his son are checking their fruit trees.

Sharing Resources

Every community member must get his or her fair share of the community's resources. This may mean making a lake for a community water supply. It may mean holding **elections** so that the people can vote on how to spend community money. Deciding how best to share resources is part of making a community a good place to live.

People in communities vote to decide how resources should be used. They choose leaders to help make these important choices.

A School Community

A school has many human resources. Each person in a school has a job to do. Students learn. Teachers teach students. The **custodian** keeps the school clean.

Desks, chairs, and books are some capital resources found in schools. Schools also need natural resources. They need water for students to drink and places for them to play.

A school librarian is an important human resource. Librarians help students to find books and look up facts.

People Helping the Community

Taking care of community resources makes a community a good place to live. People can keep natural resources clean by putting litter in trash cans. Some people help human resources by **volunteering**. They may visit sick people or gather food for the poor. People may also share capital resources. There are many ways that people help a community to succeed.

Glossary

capital resource (KA-pih-tul REE-sors) Something made by people that helps to make goods or provide services.

custodian (kuh-STOH-dee-in) A caretaker who cleans a school or other building.

elections (ee-LEK-shunz) Choosing someone for a position by voting for him or her.

goods (GUDZ) Things people make or grow that are bought by others.

human resources (HYOO-mun REE-sors-ez) The efforts of people who make goods and provide services.

natural resource (NA-chuh-rul REE-sors) Something found in nature that can be used by people.

resources (REE-sors-ez) Things that are used to provide goods and services.

rural (RUR-ul) Having to do with the country or a farming area.

services (SER-vis-ez) Work that people do for others.

suburban (suh-BER-bun) Having to do with an area of homes and businesses that is near a large city.

urban (UR-bun) Having to do with a city.

volunteering (vah-lun-TEER-ing) Working for no pay.

Index

Web Sites

Due to the changing nature of Internet links, PowerKids Press has developed an online list of Web sites related to the subject of this book. This site is updated regularly. Please use this link to access the list: www.powerkidslinks.com/caw/comresour/